By the same Author.

SEEKING FOR LIGHT:

SERMONS.

Crown 8vo. cloth, price 5*s*.

C. KEGAN PAUL & CO., 1 Paternoster Square.

THE COLLAPSE

OF

SCIENTIFIC ATHEISM

BY

J. M. WINN, M.D. M.R.C.P. &c.

AUTHOR OF

'MATERIALISM,' 'THE NATURE AND TREATMENT OF HEREDITARY DISEASE,' ETC.

Originally published in THE JOURNAL OF PSYCHOLOGICAL MEDICINE
New Series, Vol. VI., Part I.

LONDON
DAVID BOGUE, 3 ST MARTIN'S PLACE, W.C.
1880

LONDON : PRINTED BY
SPOTTISWOODE AND CO., NEW-STREET SQUARE
AND PARLIAMENT STREET

TO

DR W. A. F. BROWNE, LL.D.

EX-COMMISSIONER IN LUNACY FOR SCOTLAND

WHOSE BRILLIANT AND PROFOUND ESSAYS ON MENTAL PHILOSOPHY

HAVE SO FREQUENTLY ENRICHED THE PAGES OF THE

'JOURNAL OF PSYCHOLOGICAL MEDICINE'

This Treatise is Inscribed

WITH HIS PERMISSION

BY HIS SINCERE FRIEND

THE AUTHOR

31 HARLEY STREET, CAVENDISH SQUARE
April 1880

THE COLLAPSE

OF

SCIENTIFIC ATHEISM.

IT must be admitted by every candid and unbiassed observer who has watched the controversy between the supporters and opponents of the materialistic theories, that have so sorely perplexed the public mind during the last five years, that the fabric on which they have been reared is baseless and tottering to its fall—in other words that scientific atheism is "played out." Nevertheless, although our opponents have been completely beaten in a regular stand-up fight, they still persist, with a stubbornness worthy of a better cause, and with a strange obliviousness of facts, to oppose their light but poisoned arrows of fiction to our heavy artillery of facts; and if they will persevere in airing their dangerous dogmas in print, we are forced, at the risk of being tiresome, to bring forward again our battery of inexorable scientific truths. This is no idle boast, and we shall proceed to show, by the irresistible logic of facts, the fallacies and inconsistencies of the theories which have been arrogantly paraded by their authors, under the garb of science. To prove this position it will be necessary to pass in review many of the facts and arguments which I have from time to time published in the *Journal of Psychological Medicine.*

To the British Association for the Advancement of Science is due the unenviable distinction of having inaugurated, through their former President, Dr. Tyndall, the infidel doctrines which have of late poisoned the minds of thousands, through the medium of the public press, which has conveyed his baneful teaching even to our very thresholds, and, we fear, made shipwreck of the faith and hopes of numbers of the rising generation.

We would be the last to check the spirit of scientific inquiry, but there are scientific publications enough for the discussion of any hypotheses, however extravagant. Surely, then, the President of a public body might, for the sake of humanity, pause before loudly proclaiming to the world unverified theories, which he must be aware would, if true, subvert the fundamental principles on which all our morality and polity are based.

As an antidote to the school of false philosophy, to which the Professor belongs, I published in the *Journal of Psychological Medicine* for April 1875, a paper* containing arguments diametrically opposed to those of Dr. Tyndall and other materialists; and as they have taken, and still take, every opportunity to bring forward any hypothesis, however extravagant, in favour of materialistic infidelity, I shall have no hesitation in taking up *seriatim*, as I have done before, the chief points of scientific atheism, which have given rise to so much controversy during the last few years, for reconsideration and confutation.

Omnipotence of Atoms and Physical Forces.—Dr. Tyndall, who believes in the Almighty Atom, showed his atheistical proclivities by quoting in his ever-to-be-deplored address the following passage from Lucretius, for whom he evidently has unbounded admiration :—" If you will appreciate and keep in mind these things, Nature, free at once and rid of her haughty lords, *is seen to do all things spontaneously of herself, without the meddling of the gods.*" He also said that he saw in matter " the promise and potency of all terrestrial life." The Professor does not seem, however, to be quite satisfied of the truth of this marvellous statement, for he subsequently confessed, with an inconsistency so common with his school, that "it is not in hours of clearness and vigour this doctrine commends itself to my mind ; that in the presence of stronger and healthier thought it ever dissolves and disappears, as offering no solution of the mystery in which we dwell, and of which we form a part." By this self-contradiction he left his molecular theory unsupported ; and yet from his subsequent writings there is strong reason to fear that Dr. Tyndall has not experienced many of those lucid intervals, in which the doctrine of materialistic atheism ceases to commend itself to his mind, and it must therefore be concluded that he is still wandering in the dark and dreary region of atheism ; for, in his answer to

* *Materialism.* Subsequently published in a separate form, with Appendix, by David Bogue, No. 3 St. Martin's Place, W.C., London.

his opponents in the *Fortnightly Review*,* he dogmatically asserts that " the conclusion of pure intellect points this way [to scientific atheism] and no other!" We will proceed to show that the reasoning on which he and others attempt to establish their infidel doctrines, is, like that of the rest of the school, not the expression of pure intellect, but rather the visionary speculation of those who have allowed their judgment to fall asleep, and given unbounded reins to their fancy. We presume Dr. Tyndall would call this " the scientific use of the imagination ;" but the question at issue is of such vital importance, that the imagination, however useful in framing scientific hypotheses, must be kept in abeyance, and in the present inquiry we shall take nothing for granted at the hands of our adversaries, but rely solely on the evidence of absolute facts.

We would premise the observations which we are about to make, before entering upon details, with the fundamental axioms, that admit of no reasonable doubt, that there can be no laws without a lawgiver, and no effect without a cause. Now, all scientific atheists admit that the universe is regulated by laws, but by a strange perversion of reasoning they ignore a Lawgiver. They also deny a superintending Providence. If a clock of human construction requires careful supervision, is it incredible that the vast wheels of the universe, which revolve with more than chronometer-like precision, should require to be guided by a Being of infinite intelligence and power ? We would be the last to limit the power of the Creator, and it is quite conceivable, as has been often suggested, that the machinery of the universe was created in such a manner that it could go on for ever without further help. It is an authenticated fact† that there is a constant dissipation of energy from the sun; that its heat is constantly passing away into space, and no compensation has yet been discovered. Who can restore this lost energy save He who first called it forth ? But the Positivists believe that the so-called physical energies now in operation on the earth are all-sufficient, and do not need constant renewal, and that there is therefore no Almighty Force required above them all. But surely faith in an eternal omnipotent power is more consonant with the common sense of mankind than the atheistical doctrine that the laws and physical forces of the universe are eternal and unalterable.

* For November 1875.

† Mr. Justice Grove, the highest authority on the subject of Conservation of Energy, in his Address before the meeting of the British Association in 1866, stated that the sun and the planets were incessantly radiating heat into space, and that science had not yet shown how the energy can be restored.

The belief in a superintending and sustaining Providence is also more in harmony with man's moral nature, for it gives the consoling conviction that the Power which can restore physical energy can also give support and fresh mental vigour to fainting humanity.

If the materialist will not accept the theory of an eternal Creator, he is inevitably driven to the monstrous conclusion that atoms are all-sufficient in themselves—in fact, endowed with higher faculties than human beings—and believe with Giordano Bruno and Dr. Tyndall that, " Matter is not the mere naked *capacity* which philosophers have pictured her to be, but the universal mother who brings forth all things as the fruit of her own womb."† After this expression of opinion, it is unfair for Darwin, Tyndall, and others, when they find that they have shocked the public feeling, to say that they do believe in a God (after their own fashion). It is by the help of such an empty protest that many of their admirers, who have not time or opportunity to examine their arguments closely, are led to adopt and believe in doctrines which cannot be proved by the inductive process of reasoning. One of the most extraordinary attempts of the atomists, and one which has completely broken down, is their strange endeavour to account for animal and vegetable growth by molecular forces. The examples which were chosen to support the hypothesis were singularly unfortunate; for instance, in order to illustrate the sufficiency of matter to produce all the marvellous beauty of the vegetable world, Tyndall draws a most illogical comparison between the growth of a tree and the action of an ingenious acoustic instrument devised by Sir C. Wheatstone, which Dr. Tyndall describes in this manner : " There is an experiment, first made by Wheatstone, where the music of a piano is transferred from its sound-board, through a thin wooden rod, across several silent rooms in succession, and poured out at a distance from the instrument. The strings of the piano vibrate, not singly, but ten at a time. Every string subdivides, yielding not one note, but a dozen. All these vibrations and subvibrations are crowded together into a bit of deal not more than a quarter of a square inch in section. Yet no note is lost. Each vibration asserts its individual rights ; and all are at last shaken forth into the air by a second sound-

---

* Since writing the above, I have found in the first number of the *Modern Review*, an article by Dr. W. B. Carpenter, on *The Force Behind Nature*, in which he gives in his adherence to the principle of a superintending Providence. As he is one of the leading physiologists of the day, his recognition of a sustaining Power is a gratifying circumstance. He observes : " I deem it just as absurd and illogical to affirm that there is no place for a God in nature, originating, directing, and controlling its forces by His will, as it would be to assert that there is no place in man's body for his conscious mind."

† *Vide* Dr. Tyndall's Address at Belfast.

board, against which the distant end of the rod presses. . . . . I turn to my tree and observe its roots, its trunk, its branches, and its leaves. As the rod conveys the music, and yields it up to the distant air, so does the trunk convey the matter and the motion—the shocks and pulses, and other *vital actions* which eventually emerge in the umbrageous foliage of the tree." It requires only a small acquaintance with the first principles of acoustics and vegetable physiology to see the fallacy of this parallel. One part of it is merely an illustration of the mode in which sounds may be conveyed rapidly to a great distance, by a vibrating medium. Far different is it with the other part of the parallel—with the gradual growth of a tree, which requires for its accomplishment a variety of processes, under the control of *vital* force. Dr. Tyndall is himself driven to the necessity of using the words *vital actions*, although he denies the existence of vitality.

Another assertion of the atomists is that vital actions are almost as physical as those that lead to the coalescence of two globules of oil suspended in a mixture of alcohol and water, which do not unite until the pellicles that have formed around them burst. From similar combinations, mounting up step by step, from one to another, it was imagined that a living body was constructed. Had the atomists recognised the wonderful facts revealed by the microscope, which some physicists are apt to despise, they would have perceived that the oil globules, with their pellicles, are totally different from the germinating cells of which a living body is built up. The original and profound observations with the microscope by Dr. Lionel Beale have shown beyond contradiction that these minute cells have the powers of absorption, motion, and proliferation, and are, in fact, true living germs, admitting of " no analogy to any non-living matter whatever."*

An equally improbable hypothesis was brought forward by Professor Huxley, who thought that a crystal and a living structure were analogous, and that both were the result of physical forces. A chemist can produce a crystal by various combinations; he can dissolve it, and afterwards reproduce it by evaporation, which cannot be done with any animal or vegetable organism. There is not the slightest resemblance between the minutest living being and a grain of salt, and a crystal as much resembles a life-cell as an icicle does a warm, living, palpitating animal.

We must then come to the inevitable conclusion that the molecular theory of life has completely broken down, and that life, this birth, this growth, this mystery which we cannot com-

* *Vide* Dr. Lionel Beale's Lumleian Lectures *On Life and on Vital Action of Health and Disease.* J. and A. Churchill, London, 1875.

prehend must have been superadded to matter after the cre
of the earth.

Bathybius.—Little need be said respecting this y
pretender. He never had the ghost of a fact to suppo
claims, and has very properly been disowned by his own pe
A year since, I made the following observation respecting
*lusus naturæ**: "Of all the ephemeral pseudo-philos
discoveries, the one which a short time since most alarme
sober thinking people and delighted the scientific atheist
Huxley's—that life sprang from deep sea mud. Huxley n
his wonderful discovery, out of compliment to Häckel, B
bius Häckelii. The joy of Strauss was without bounds.
was the link that was needed to join the organic with
inorganic world, and the superstitious belief in a Creato
received its death-blow. This is what he says, in *The Old*
and the New†: '*Huxley has discovered* the bathybius, a
heap of jelly on the sea bottom; Häckel what he has calle
moneres, structureless clots of an albuminous carbon, v
although inorganic in their constitution, yet are capal
nutrition and accretion. By these the chasm may be said
bridged, and the transition effected from the inorganic t
organic.' Since this was written Huxley himself has aband
the muddy notion of bathybius."

Spontaneous Generation.—This extraordinary idea, op
to all experience, which had, strange to say, some enthus
supporters, even among men of science, two years ago
vanished into thin air. It is singular that we shoul
indebted to Dr. Tyndall, the high priest of Materialism, fo
complete contradiction of this materialistic figment. I
one must admit that the Professor is almost unequalled a
experimenter; and we must not forget our obligations to
for so candidly exposing the fallacies of a theory that would
given so much support to the creed which he unfortun
upholds. He published a full and faithful report of his ex
ments in the *Nineteenth Century* for January 1877. He 1
a thousand experiments on infusions of vegetable matter, he
to a temperature sufficiently high to destroy all vital organ
and he found that no sign of life could be discovered in a
them, unless by any chance external air, containing gern
matter, had been admitted. Virchow, the eminent ph
logist, confirms Dr. Tyndall's observations. I quote his ren
as they appeared in the *Times*: "Moreover the *gene*
equivoca which has been so often contested, and so often co
dicted, is nevertheless always meeting us afresh. To be sur

---

* *Vide* an article on *Modern Pseudo-Philosophy*—*Journal of Psycho*
Medicine, vol. iv., part I. New Series.
† *The Old Faith and the New*, p. 188. Asker & Co.. London, 1873.

know not a single positive fact to prove that *a generatio equivoca* has ever been made—that there ever has been procreation in this way; that inorganic masses such as Carbon and Co. have ever spontaneously developed themselves into organic masses. Nevertheless, I grant that if anyone is determined to form for himself an idea of how the first organic being could come into existence of itself, nothing further is left than to go back to spontaneous generation. This much is evident. If I do not choose to accept a theory of creation; if I refuse to believe that there was a special Creator who took the clod of earth and breathed into it the breath of life; if I prefer to make for myself a verse after my own fashion (in the place of the verse in Genesis), then I must make it in the sense of *generatio equivoca. Tertium non datur.* No alternative remains when once we say ' I do not accept the creation, but I will have an explanation.' Whoever takes up that first position, must go on to the second position and say ;—'*Ergo,* I assume the *generatio equivoca.*' But of this we do not possess any actual proof. No one has ever seen a *generatio equivoca* really effected, and whoever supposes that it has occurred is contradicted by the naturalist and not merely by the theologian."

In the face of these facts, who will be so bold as to believe in spontaneous generation?

Evolution.—It is a melancholy satire on the credulity of mankind that this unverified theory of pseudo-philosophy should have taken such a firm hold on the minds not only of numerous laymen, but also of some weak-minded or faint-hearted clergymen. With a timidity unworthy of their creed—which has been glorified by the blood of the noble army of martyrs and the heroic deeds of the Crusaders—men of high position in the Church are endeavouring to reconcile it with the atheistical doctrine of evolution, and making a miserable attempt to adapt Christianity to Darwinism, instead of fighting manfully, not only against the world and the flesh, but also against evolution. They imagine that all may be made smooth by admitting that the primordial germ was created—not produced—by spontaneous generation or the potentiality of atoms. They do not seem to be aware that if they admit that the first germ was created millions of years ago, and was sufficient to develop all the endless and complicated forms of life which are found at the present day upon the earth, it must follow that the necessity for a watchful and superintending Providence is done away with. This Theistic form of evolution removes the Creator so far from us and our sympathies that He becomes a mere vanishing point in the dim vista of infinity. They have recently had recourse to another expedient. They attempt to draw a line between the evolution of animals and the origin of man. The latter, they say, was produced by a special creation, the former by development. This is virtually a surrender at discretion, for if evolution could produce all the animals in the world, why not man?

It is a mistaken policy for the clergy to succumb to their antagonists at the present time, when the discoveries of science are more than ever opposed to the fatalistic doctrine of Darwinism in every form. The advocates of evolution are constantly driven to make concessions, and its most sanguine supporters do not pretend to say that they can establish it by the inductive process of reasoning. Nevertheless, a writer in the *Nineteenth Century*, so recently as December 1879, has the boldness to say, " The grand scientific hypothesis (evolution) of the century is upon its trial, as the theories of Newton and Galileo were before it!"

I will now proceed to array against the chimera of evolution the phalanx of facts which strike at its very root. In 1875, in the essay to which I previously referred, I adduced some of the facts which show that evolution, which *assumes to be a law*, is absolutely at *variance* with the *recognised laws of nature*. I there stated that no one has succeeded in producing a new genus or a decidedly new species, though it is well known to all breeders of animals—and to every common gardener—that an enormous variety of animals and plants can be produced by careful selection, crossing, &c. Long before Darwin's work on *The Descent of Man* appeared, naturalists had observed the gradations of organisms, on which evolutionists lay so much stress, as well as the similarity of the bodily functions and conformations of animals; but this is nothing more than that *archetypal unity*, which is found throughout all nature.

The barrenness of hybrids is universally acknowledged, and is utterly irreconcilable with the theory of evolution. Can a better reason be given than the one commonly received, that the great Lawgiver has established a *law* to prevent the confusion of species?

In the same essay I stated the fact that the forms and features of men and animals are the same now as they were thousands of years ago, as depicted on the Egyptian monuments, or as still traceable in the mummies of the pyramids, and that the intellect of man has never been developed in a higher degree than it was in the days of the Hebrew prophets and Greek poets. The only answer offered is, that evolution requires not only thousands, but billions upon billions of years for the development of a new species. This is dreaming and not sober reasoning. The palæontologists can read the records of the past, stamped on the crust of the earth, but who can read the future of a million years to come? The mind of man has not only a limited field of observation, but has also limits to its own power, and it is not a healthy exercise for the mind to indulge overmuch in the pleasures of the imagination.

The periods required for the evolution of one species into another are infinitely longer than the time, as calculated by the physicists, which has elapsed since life first appeared on the face of the earth. It has been estimated that a period not much exceeding one hundred millions of years must have passed since the earth was sufficiently cooled down to support life. An approximate calculation will show that this is not nearly long enough for the imaginary law of evolution to produce all the species, living and extinct, that have been discovered; for the Darwinites are obliged to admit that a time almost fabulous is required for the development of even a single species by evolution.

Sir Charles Lyell estimated the now existing species of vegetables and animals on the terraqueous globe at one and a half millions: this is exclusive of microscopic beings, whose number is incalculable. A single drop of stagnant water, according to Leeuwenhoeck, contains about 500,000,000 of animalcules, a large number of which probably consists of distinct species. Sir Charles Lyell says it is very difficult to form a calculation of the number of extinct species. Each stratum which contains fossils is marked by species which are peculiar to it and to the epoch when they were deposited, and myriads have no doubt been obliterated by the mechanical and chemical forces to which they have been subjected.

It may be roughly calculated, from the observations of various naturalists and geologists, that the number of extinct species, including both animals and vegetables, amounts to not less than 3,000,000. The addition of 1,500,000 of still existing species makes a total of 4,500,000. If we grant for the sake of argument, that one species could be evolved from another in so short a space of time as 5,000 years, and multiply the 4,500,000 species, living and extinct, by 5,000, we shall find the time required to produce all the number of species that have ever appeared is 22,500,000,000.

Difficulties are constantly arising in the path of the evolutionist. Can he inform us whence, or through what channel, the nightingale derives her song? Are the wings of birds derived from the quills of the porcupine? Whence does the beaver obtain his constructive power, the spider learn to spin her geometric web, or the carrier pigeon acquire her wonderful instinct? Are the beauty and scent of flowers, which are the grace and ornament of the earth, due to natural selection?

The habits of different kinds of bees have been quoted in proof of this law of natural selection, showing that the skill of the house-bee has been developed by evolution, step by step, through inferior classes of bees. It is also believed regarding instinct, that it is to be accounted for by hereditary transmission; that each animal is "not individually taught, its personal experience is *nil*, but has the benefit of ancestral experience. In that inherited organisation are registered all the powers which it displays at birth." In this manner the chick learns "the very complex co-ordination of eye, muscles, and beak" which enable it, on "coming out of the egg, to balance itself correctly, run about, pick up its food" &c. In all cases of this kind the evolutionist holds that the instinctive powers displayed by animals are nothing more than the results of organic memory. The law of hereditary transmission cannot be disputed, but it is carried to a fabulous length when it is asserted that the human brain is a register of "infinitely numerous experiences received during the evolution of that series of organisms through which the human organism has been reached." But all this ingenious speculation must not be mistaken for sober truth, and when we show, as we hope to do, that the organic chain, which is supposed to support this airy fabric, is destitute, not only of what should have been its strongest link—the ape-man, but is also wanting in many other links, it must be acknowledged that the dream of evolution will pass away like the "baseless fabric of a vision."

Two years since, having seen no answer to the above difficulties in the way of Darwinism, I repeated them in an article which I published in the *Journal of Psychological Medicine*,[*] and gave the following additional evidence of its fallacy, from two of the highest authorities in natural history and palæontology. Mr. William Carruthers said, in his address delivered at the opening of the Geologists' Association in November 1875 [†]:—"The plants portrayed on the ancient paintings and sculptures of Egypt; the fruits placed in coffins with embalmed bodies, and the fruits and seeds found in ancient lake dwellings, all belong to existing species, with which they agree in the most minute and apparently accidental particulars. The existing order of plants *if it be due to genetic evolution supplies no proof of it*. . . . The cellular algæ preceded the vascular cryptogams, or the gymnosperms of the newer palæozoic rocks, and these were speedily followed by monoctyledons, and at a much later period by dicotyledons. But the earliest representatives of those various sections of the vegetable kingdom

---

* *Modern Pseudo-Philosophy*, vol. iv., part I. New Series.
† By William Carruthers, Esq., F.R.S., F.L.S., F.G.S., &c., Keeper of the Botanical Department of the British Museum.

are not generalised forms, but as highly organised as recent forms, and in many cases _more highly organised_; and the divisions were as clearly bounded in their essential characters, and as decidedly separated from each other as they are at the present day. . . . Is it possible from the record of organic life preserved in the sedimentary deposits, to discover the method or agent through the action of which the new forms appeared on the globe? The rocks record the existence of the plants and animal forms, but as yet they have disclosed nothing whatever as to _how_ these forms originated."

The testimony of Thomas Davidson, Esq., F.R.S., V.P.P.S., &c., derived from the animal kingdom, is equally strong. Mr. Davidson is one of the most distinguished palæontologists of the age, few men having had more honours bestowed on them from both British and foreign scientific bodies. He stands unrivalled in his knowledge of the nature and history of those small seashells called brachiopoda, of which there are three thousand species. He is, moreover, the friend of Darwin, and it was at the particular request of that great naturalist that he undertook the task of minutely examining the characteristics of the brachiopods, with a view of proving whether or not they would support the truth of the Darwinian theory. In the _Geological Magazine_ for 1877 Mr. Davidson says: " We have no positive evidence of those modifications which the theory invokes, for types appear on the whole to be permanent as long as they continue, and when a genus disappears there is no modification that I can see of any of the forms that continue beyond, as far as the brachiopoda appear to be concerned ; and why should a number of genera, such as lingula, discina, crania, and rhynchonella have continued to be represented with the same characters, and often with but small modification in shape during the entire sequence of geological strata? Why did they not offer modifications or alter during those incalculable ages? Limiting myself to the brachiopoda, let us see what further they will tell us on this question. Taking the present state of our knowledge as a guide, but admitting at the same time that any day our conclusions and inductions may require to be modified by fresh discoveries, let us ascertain whether they reveal anything to support Darwinian ideas. We find that the larger number of genera made their first appearance during the palæozoic periods, and since they have been decreasing in number to the present period. We will leave out of the question the species, for they vary so little that it is often very difficult to trace really good distinctive characters between them ; it is different with the genera, as they are, or should be, founded on much greater and more permanent distinctions. Thus, for example, the family Spiriferidæ includes genera which are all characterised by a calcified spiral lamina for the support of the drachial appendages; and, however varied these may be, they always retain the distinctive characters of the group from their first appearance to their extinction. . . . Now, although certain genera, such as terebratala, rhynchonella, crania, and discina have enjoyed a very considerable geological existence there are genera, such as stringocephalus, uncites, porambonites, koninckina, and several others, which made their appearance very suddenly and without any warning; after a while they disappeared in a similar abrupt manner, having enjoyed a comparatively short existence. They are all possessed of such marked and distinctive internal characters that we cannot trace between them and associated or synchronous genera any evidence of their being the result of descent with modification." It is thus evident that the eminent brachiopodist, to whom Darwin himself had referred for the confirmation of his theory, has decided against him.

I also drew attention at the same time to the facts, that the fossil trilobite crops up *abruptly*, at the close of the carboniferous epoch, with *the eye perfectly developed*—that no breeding has yet been able to produce, by selection, two species so distinct that they can generate hybrids—and that there is a limit to the variability of species. The scientific objections to the Darwinian hypothesis are innumerable, and its advocates are constantly driven to fresh concessions. It would be well if its supporters would be silent for a while. A fixed law or a general principle gains by investigation, but this has not been the case with Darwinism. Every year some fresh defect is revealed, and it is wonderful that there should still remain any who believe it to be standing on as firm a basis as the law of gravitation. Häckel goes so far as to propose that it should be accepted as the basis of education! and " the protoplastic soul (*die plastidul-seele*) be assumed as the foundation of all ideas concerning spiritual being!" Can this extravagance be exceeded?

We are indebted to Dr. Bateman for a valuable work, *Darwinism tested by Language*,* in which he proves scientifically, that the faculty of language places an impassable gulf between man and the brute creation. This work was very unpalatable to evolutionists, and Dr. Bucknill, in a review of it, in the first number of *Brain*, not being able to refute this fact, had recourse to the dangerous expedient of attempting to turn his opponent into ridicule, by stating that he was unable to comprehend the " amount of evidence " which " Darwin had collected " in favour

* Rivingtons, London.

of evolution. To us it appears, on the contrary, that Dr. Bucknill himself does not appreciate, or is "not aware of the amount of evidence" on the other side of the question. In my review of *Brain*, in the *Journal of Psychological Medicine*,* I asked him to answer the objections which we have already advanced in the foregoing pages. I will now give a few extra—additional facts, and if they all remain unanswered the inference must be—that they are unanswerable.

It has been asserted that the distinguishing characteristics observed in animals in various countries are due to their environments—to use a newly-coined word. How does it happen then, that in parts of South Africa and Australia, alike in soil and climate, the species are entirely different?

Evolutionists have never informed us which was developed first, the male or the female of animals. A man and woman are very different, and yet one mother produces both. How can this be? Again, how is the balance of the sexes preserved? These are mysteries which the materialist can no more explain than he can the mystery of life.

It is impossible for the evolutionists to explain by insensible gradations or fortuitous changes the orign of the electric battery in the torpedo. Would they presume to say that if Galvani was able to perfect his battery in a few years, the Great Mechanician required billions of years to complete the wonderful weapon of defence with which the torpedo is endowed?

Another point on which great stress has been laid, is the resemblance in appearance between the human embryo, and that of various animals, during its development in utero. But a little consideration will show that the similarity is partial, and is not carried so far as to lead to any doubt as to the existence of that law which prevents the confusion of species; and without which the world would long ago have been filled with legions of monstrosities.

It is affirmed that the human embryo, when in utero, passes through successive forms of organisation analogous to those of a fish, a reptile, a bird, and the inferior mammalia. But if it is fish-like at one period of its growth, how does it not sometimes come to pass that it is developed into a perfect fish. There must be a fundamental difference between the germ of a man and that of a fish from the very beginning, which no microscope has yet been able to detect. Moreover, psychological observations have led to the probable inference that the brain of the human fœtus, does not at any time exactly resemble that of any inferior animal. Merely vague resemblances are very imperfect data on which to form a theory.

* *Vide Journal of Psychological Medicine.* New Series, vol. iv., part II.

With reference to the two principles—"the struggle for existence" and "selection in relation to sex"—nothing more need be said here, than that they would be of no avail with regard to those animals that are destitute of the power of locomotion.

We have mentioned facts enough, and more than enough, to prove that the chain of evidence in favour of evolution, which was supposed to be constructed of links of iron, is in truth no better than a rope of sand. Much of its popularity was due to its advocacy by Herbert Spencer, and other Positivists, who no doubt were delighted to find a theory which gave support to their atheistical opinions. It is extraordinary that the illogical lucubrations which Herbert Spencer disseminated under the garb of philosophy should have been received with such admiration, not only by a portion of the public, but also by scientific men, like Dr. Tyndall and Dr. Allen Thomson. The former called him the "Apostle of the Understanding." Does he think that what Herbert Spencer says of life, which he defines as "a continuous adjustment of internal relations to external relations," has won that title for him? Can anything be more indefinite than such a definition? I would ask, has he originated or established any great scientific or moral truth?* Again I repeat that as a writer he is obscure and pedantic, and his style forms a striking contrast to the simplicity and perspicuity of our greatest writers. This is what he says of evolution: "Evolution is a change from indefinite incoherent homogeneity to a definite coherent heterogeneity, through continuous differentiations and integrations." This is little short of nonsense. Can such expressions as these be considered indications of a master mind, and is such a teacher to be looked up to as a guiding star?

One of the evil fruits of evolution is the objection it has raised to the evidences of "design in nature"—a theme which has given rise to the holiest thoughts and called forth the noblest expressions of adoration and praise. We have now to learn that the admirable Bridgwater Treatises, by Sir Charles Bell and others, are mistakes, and that the prosaic process of development effects all that is seen in animated nature, and that we are to shut our eyes to the endless wonders of design, as exhibited by the manner in which the requirements of the species are suited to the circumstances in which they are placed. Are not the wings of the eagle adapted for an elevated

* We must apologise. We had nearly forgotten the great discovery he has recently announced—that it is the duty of man to enjoy himself. This establishes his fame, not only as the "Apostle of the Understanding," but as one of the greatest moralists of the age. Some have illnaturedly remarked that it is to Epicurus, and not to Herbert Spencer, we are indebted for this great moral truth.

flight, and the fins of the trout to darting through the water ? *

Beauty can have no place in the scheme of the evolutionist, for it is impossible to believe that the lowest grades of animals acquired it by the assumed law of natural selection. One of the greatest of living geniuses (Ruskin) says the Power which gave to "the opal its fire," which "wreathed the swan with snow and bathed the dove with iridescence," would not be subdued under the slow influence of accident and time.† Genius spurns evolution—common sense ridicules it.‡

* To Dr. Andrew Wilson we are indebted for the following striking instance of design: "Even more interesting than the case of the primrose is that of the myosotis versicolor, a species of forget-me-not, the arrangement for securing fertilisation of the seed exhibiting a perfect adaptation to all possible exigencies which may arise in the life history of the flower. If we examine the myosotis just after the flower has opened, the pistil with its long style is seen to project above the level of the flower itself. It thus presents a most likely object for contact with the proboscis of an insect which has come from another myosotis laden with pollen. But failing to obtain fertilisation of its seeds by insect-carried pollen from a neighbour flower, the myosotis has yet another resource in the pollen of its own stamens. The stamens at the opening of the flower are placed far below the style, and hence it is impossible, so long as the stamens remain below, for the pollen to be placed on the pistil and thus to fertilise the seeds. But nature has been equal to such an emergency. As time passes, we find the stamens to grow upwards with the petals, and as in time they overtop the pistil, the flower is enabled to fertilise its own seeds. Not less interesting or remarkable are the phases observed in the action of pollen itself, in its work of fertilisation. Left to themselves and unapplied to their special purpose, the little yellow grains of pollen wither and die. But, placed in its appropriate and intended situation on the pistil, each pollen grain, as if guided by some inherent instinct, projects from its surface a tube-like structure, which passes through the style of the pistil, and brings the essential matters of the pollen grain in contact with the seeds"

† From Ruskin's *Love's Meinie*, in a lecture on Greek and English birds. G. Allen & Co., Keston, Kent, 1873.

‡ The following satire appeared originally in an American paper a few years since. I never could learn the name of the paper, or of the writer. It is too good to be lost sight of:—

"The New Scriptures, according to Tyndall and others.

"1. Primarily the Unknowable moved upon cosmos and evolved protoplasm.

"2. And protoplasm was inorganic and undifferentiated, containing all things in potential energy; and a spirit of evolution moved upon the fluid mass.

"3. And the Unknowable said, Let atoms attract; and their contact begat light, heat, and electricity.

"4. And the unconditioned differentiated the atoms, each after its kind; and their combinations begat rock, air, and water.

"5. And there went out a spirit of evolution from the Unconditioned, and, working in protoplasm by accretion and absorption, produced the organic cell.

"6. And cell, by nutrition, evolved primordial germ, and germ developed protogene, and protogene begat eozoon, and eozoon begat monad, and monad begat animalcule.

"7. And animalcule begat ephemera; then began creeping things to multiply on the face of the earth.

"8. And earthly atom in vegetable protoplasm begat the molecule, and thence came all grass and every herb in the earth.

"9. And animalcula in the water evolved fins, tails, claws, and scales; and in the air, wings and beaks; and on the land they sprouted such organs as were necessary as played upon by the environment.

Anyone who visits the Zoological Gardens, in a healthy frame of mind, cannot fail to be struck with the evidences of design as exhibited in the conformation of the various animals, so marvellously adapted to the spheres in which they were born, each one having been so organised as to be fitted to get his own " living, in that state of life in which it had pleased God "—not evolution—to place him.*

Many of those who adopt evolution as a guiding principle have been driven into a complete state of puzzledom. The Rev. J. W. Fowle, in the *Nineteenth Century* for July 1878,

" 10. And by accretion and absorption came the radiata and mollusca, and mollusca begat articulata, and articulata begat vertebrata.

" 11. Now these are the generations of the higher vertebrata, in the cosmic period that the Unknowable evoluted the bipedal mammalia.

" 12. And every man of the earth, while he was yet a monkey, and the horse, while he was a hipparion, and the hipparion, before he was an oredon.

" 13. Out of the ascidian came the amphibian, and begat the pentadactyle, and the pentadactyle by inheritance and selection produced the hylobate, from which are the simiadæ in all their tribes.

" 14. And out of the simiadæ the lemur prevailed above his fellows and produced the platyrhine monkey.

" 15. And the platyrhine begat the catarrhine, and the catarrhine monkey begat the anthropoid ape, and the ape begat the longimanous ourang, and the ourang begat the chimpanzee, and the chimpanzee evoluted the what-is-it.

" 16. And the what-is-it went into the land of Nod and took him a wife of the longimanous gibbons.

" 17. And in process of the cosmic period were born unto them and their children the anthropomorphic primordial types.

" 18. The homunculus, the prognathus, the troglodyte, the autochthon, the terragen—these are the generations of primeval man.

" 19. And primeval man was naked and not ashamed, but lived in quadrumanous innocence, and struggled mightily to harmonise with the environment.

" 20. And by inheritance and natural selection did he progress from the stable and homogeneous to the complex and heterogeneous ; for the weakest died, and the strongest grew and multiplied.

" 21. And man grew a thumb, for that he had need of it, and developed capacities for prey.

" 22. For, behold, the swiftest men caught the most animals, and the swiftest animals got away from the most men ; wherefore the slow animals were eaten, and the slow men starved to death.

" 23. And as types were differentiated, the weaker types continually disappeared.

" 24. And the earth was filled with violence, for man strove with man, and tribe with tribe, whereby they killed off the weak and foolish, and secured the survival of the fittest."

* It may be here incidentally noticed that some men of high culture have been saddened by the thought that the progress of modern science has reduced both the earth and man to greater insignificance. Astronomy, by extending our view of the universe, and navigation, by enabling us to steam round the globe in a holiday tour, have, they say, given a familiarity and comparative contempt for the earth and for ourselves. But if astronomy has added *trillions* of miles to our knowledge of the space between us and distant suns, our *idea* of infinite space is not increased any more than when we thought they were only *billions* of miles from us ; and our more intimate acquaintance with the geography of the earth does not lower our position, or make us less the lords of the brute creation. The multiplicity of stars need not discomfort us, if Coleridge's idea be true. When asked what could be the use of so many worlds if they were uninhabited, he replied. " To make dirt cheap.'"

labours hard to find a place in it for conscience! Another poor bewildered writer in the *North American Review* cries aloud for a new religion.

Spiritualists, by a strange anomaly, talk of materialising spirits; and one of their body has lately said that the last step of evolution is to develop the human spirit. The force of evolution can no further go—it is played out.

Antiquity of Man.—The subdued tone of the believers in the fabulous antiquity of man, at the last meeting of the British Association, at Sheffield, was a strong contrast to the boldness and confidence with which Mr. Pengelly, F.R.S., delivered a sensational address on the previous occasion, at Glasgow, to a crowded audience. Mr. Pengelly was one of those who were selected by the Royal Society to examine the contents of the Brixham Cavern. It is therefore to be regretted that, on insufficient evidence, he should have availed himself of the influence of his position to imbue the public mind with the notion that the facts revealed by the exploration of the Brixham Cavern proved the existence of man in Devon during the pre-glacial, or at least inter-glacial period. The chief evidence is derived from the discovery of what he terms flint implements and a stone hammer in the cavern. It is fair that the public should know what has been said on the other side of the question.

Mr. Whitley, Vice-President of the Royal Institution of Cornwall, whose talent, enthusiasm, and geological attainments are not inferior to those of Mr. Pengelly, has made most careful examinations of the Brixham Cavern, and his deductions are diametrically opposed to those of the former gentleman. In several papers which he read before the " Victoria Institute, or Philosophical Society of Great Britain," Mr. Whitley has proved that the supposed flint implements are not of human manufacture, and are nothing more than pieces of rubble flint and fragmentary flakes that had drifted into the cavern, and he adduced good evidence to prove that they had a geological and not an antiquarian origin. He stated that, if a nodule of flint be crushed by a heavy blow, it will shiver into flakes precisely similar to those found in the cavern, and, moreover, that change of temperature will split silicious minerals into flake, resembling the supposed knives and scrapers.

Mr. Whitley, in an exhaustive treatise, entitled, *A Critical Examination of the Flints from Brixham Cavern*,* gives the following summary of his arguments :—

" I have now shown that the so-called ' thirty-six rude flint implements, of indisputable human workmanship,' are, for the

* *A Critical Examination of the Flints from Brixham Cavern.* David Bogue, 3 St. Martin's Place, London, W.C. 1877.

greatest part, small undefinable pieces of rubble flint, mixed with a few imperfect subsoil flakes.

"That the marks of use, or secondary chipping, so strongly asserted to be found on the edges of the flints, and so clearly shown on the woodcut, fig. 410, in *Ancient Stone Implements*, are not to be found on the flint itself.

"That the flint described in *Ancient Stone Implements* as a remarkably symmetrical scraper, and said to be found in the cavern, was not found there but in the soil without and above it.

"That the cast of a very perfect flint knife exhibited among other relics in the cavern, and sold to visitors as a cast of a cavern specimen, is a deception.

"That the portion of a cylindrical pin or rod of ivory, said to be found in the cave, was not found by the committee of exploration, is not now with the flints in the museum, and that there is no evidence to show that it is a cavern specimen.

"That the 'charcoal bed' contains no charcoal. That slate has been mistaken for flint, and flint for bone; and that the description given of the 'whole hind-leg of a cave bear,' the most famous specimen of the cavern, has been found to be so loaded with erroneous facts and false conclusions, that its evidence has been withdrawn and abandoned."

With regard to the so-called stone hammer, Mr. Prestwich is of opinion that it is a Budleigh-Salterton pebble; and Mr. Whitley observes that it was imbedded in drifted gravel similar to that of the neighbouring raised beaches. He contends that it was introduced into the cavern by natural causes, and that the indentations on its surface, which have been regarded as signs of its having been used as a hammer, are due to its having been "battered by a thousand storms."

Southall, the eminent American geologist, in his work on the *Recent Origin of Man** gives it as his opinion that the earliest inhabitants of western Europe were intelligent savages, like the Esquimaux Indians, and that neither archæology nor geology have detected any earlier form of man. We may therefore hesitate to believe that the aborigines of Devon were no better than beasts, who herded with wild animals in dens and caves. He mentions a curious fact, which shows how cautious observers who have pet theories should be not to jump to hasty conclusions. A skull said to have been found in a cave was pronounced by Huxley to be a most brutal human skull. It was afterwards discovered, on careful examination, to be an average skull. Moreover, it was not associated with extinct animals, and was discovered under five feet of mud! In

* *Recent Origin of Man*. Philadelphia, 1875. Trübner & Co., London.

the face of these facts, the *Illustrated London News* for August 25 last, in the report of Mr. Pengelly's paper, confidently assures us that the "discovery and systematic exploration of a comparatively small virgin cavern on Windmill Hill, at Brixham (in 1858), led to a sudden and complete revolution, for it was seen that, whatever were the facts elsewhere, there had undoubtedly been found at Brixham flint implements, commingled with remains of the mammoth and its companions, and in such a way as to render it impossible to doubt that man occupied Devonshire before the extinction of the mammoth."

With all the evidence to the contrary, it seems certain, in spite of all Mr. Pengelly says, that this Orson—this wild man of the caves—this grovelling monster—never inhabited the caverns of Devon; and we have yet to learn that any other part of the world had the honour of being his birthplace.

Physiological Psychology.—This pseudo-science, which was ushered in with such loud and triumphant acclamations, and was supposed by its enthusiastic supporters to solve the mystery of mind—this *ignis fatuus* which, if true, would destroy the independence of the mind and the freedom of the human will—has at length proved to be nothing more than a wild and visionary speculation.

Physiological psychology is the most subtle and dangerous form of scientific atheism, because the knowledge required to confute it is confined to a limited number of inquirers. Its doctrines are permeating all classes of society, and are most conspicuous among the younger members of the medical profession; which is to be expected when so many of the influential teachers, holding high rank in our medical schools, have unhesitatingly and recklessly done their utmost to imbue the minds of the rising generation of students with the notion that all our time-honoured creeds are the assumptions of credulity and folly. The students are taught to look down upon them with contempt, and to substitute speculative opinions, which cannot be of the slightest practical value, but must inevitably, sooner or later, make shipwreck of the highest hopes and noblest aspirations of our nature.

I stated five years ago in the *Journal of Psychological Medicine*, and again in an address on the *Materialistic Physiology*, which I delivered before the Victoria Institute, in 1877, that the terms Mental Physiology and Physiological Psychology were illogical and anomalous, as they jumbled together mind and matter, and I proposed to substitute the term *Materialistic Physiology.** I also stated that the chief dogma

* Subsequently published in *The Journal of Psychological Medicine*. Vol. iii., Part I.

of the new school is that mind and all its faculties—perception, memory, will, reason, imagination, as well as all moral attributes—are the result of bodily functions, as if they were secretions from the brain, like those of the liver or kidneys. They have various unintelligible modes of describing the phenomena of the mind. Its operations are spoken of by some as the product of the caudate cells of the brain—by others as a disturbance of the equilibrium of the nervous power—as expressions of material changes in the brain—as cerebral vibration—an emanation from the body, &c.* It seems strange that anyone can believe, or expect others to believe, that assertions like these, unverified by careful scientific inductions, can be substituted for what is commonly understood by the word " mind." Mind is a fact; its existence is proved by our own consciousness, and its operations are indelibly inscribed on the literature and art of ages. It would be as absurd to doubt it as to doubt that of a God, although we cannot explain the nature of either. That it is connected in a mysterious manner with our organisation no one can disbelieve, but we defy the modern physiologists to explain the connection. They speak as confidently of their speculative opinions as if they were acknowledged facts, and as if recent researches had thrown a flood of light on the functions of the brain and spinal cord. I again challenge them, as I have done before, to show that any one really great fact has been elicited since the discoveries of Sir Charles Bell and Marshall Hall. The nerve-fibres of sensation and motion have been traced a little further towards the circumference of the brain, but we are as ignorant as ever of the properties of the caudate nerve-cells of the cerebral convolutions; we can only surmise that it is through them that sensations are perceived and volition exercised.

The chief arguments which have been brought forward in favour of materialistic physiology may be summed up as follows :—

First. That the doctrine of a correlation of force proves that vital, and even mental energy, are interchangeable with physical force.

Secondly. That the phenomena of insanity give weight to the theory of physiological psychology.

Thirdly. That memory is merely a register of impressions on the brain cells.

* The English language itself is getting corrupted by the new philosophical nomenclature that has been adopted in the endeavour to make the new theories intelligible. They will soon require to publish a glossary of the new terms which are accumulating fast. For instance, they call poetic emotion the thrill of a ganglion; thought, cerebration; life, molecular force; creation, evolution; the Deity, a primordial germ; crime, cerebral disease; &c.

Fourthly. That there is a function of the brain, termed unconscious cerebration, by which it is understood that the brain can think without individual consciousness.

Fifthly. That the experiments of Fritsch, Hitzig, Ferrier, &c., have gone far to prove that mental faculties can be localised in the brain.

Although the last of the points which we have enumerated, we will take first into consideration the recent electrical experiments on the brain, especially as they just now occupy so much attention both at home and abroad, particularly among the members of the medical profession.

One of the most prominent teachers of this mode of investigation, in this country, is Dr. Ferrier; my observations will therefore be chiefly directed to his experiments and deductions.

With an incomprehensible alacrity, the medical journals in England, with scarcely an exception, vied with each other in extolling Dr. Ferrier to the skies; they seemed to think that he had discovered a royal road to a thorough knowledge of the nature of the human mind—it was nothing more, after all, than a mass of cerebral functions. They did not stop to consider that the inevitable consequence of that belief must be, that mind and brain would both perish together. A pleasant prospect, if true!

In my address before the Victoria Institute in 1877 I remarked that physiological psychology was the revival of the exploded system of phrenology, under a new name. Its object is to materialise mind, by giving a local habitation to each of the moral and intellectual faculties in different parts of the brain. The scheme is an old one, and has been defeated over and over again; nevertheless, as time goes on, it is revived in some fresh shape, either by those who think, by the adaptation of a new phraseology to an old idea, they can gain reputation and fame, or by well-meaning but too enthusiastic men, whose imaginations are unfortunately stronger than their reason; men who, however distinguished in some special department of natural science, are evidently incapacitated by their mental constitution from clearly comprehending the fundamental truths of psychology.

It is the confident boast of this psycho-physiological school that the physiological method is the only means of arriving at a right interpretation of mental phenomena; that it is by experiments on the brain, combined with a careful study of the functions of the nervous system, that it will be ultimately proved that mind is only a function of the brain, and that all the great metaphysical truths which have been believed and taught for thousands of years are to be regarded as idle tales.

Dr. Ferrier has published two works* in which he gave an account of his observations and experiments. I reviewed them both, one in October 1877 and the other in April 1879,† and combated his deductions from them, especially with reference to the localisation of *mental* faculties in the brain.

As the experiments which Dr. Ferrier, Fritsch, Hitzig, and others conducted were performed on the brains of monkeys, cats, dogs, jackals, rabbits, pigeons, frogs, and fish, we would remark, in the first place, that we cannot conceive, even if they had been less conflicting, how they would throw any light on the nature of the moral or intellectual faculties of man.

It so happens that Brown-Sequard and Eugène Dupuy (of New York) cerebral physiologists holding the highest rank, and most careful experimenters, have come to conclusions diametrically opposed to the above authorities. Five years since I remarked in the *Journal of Psychological Medicine* that " many of the so-called discoveries of the most painstaking cerebral physiologists are at variance with each other. It had been for a long time believed that the optic thalami were closely connected with the upper extremities as motor centres, but experiments by Northangel had completely dislocated our ideas on the point, for he found that, after destroying the whole of the optic thalami, rabbits were able to leap about. These facts show that physiologists should pause before asserting that the highest mental manifestations are only emanations from particular portions of the brain, when they have not yet been able to satisfactorily determine the centres of motion and sensation."

Dr. Ferrier's experiments consisted, first in ploughing up (as he expresses it) parts of the brain by a wire cautery; secondly, in wholesale slicing away large portions of the cerebral substance; and thirdly, in electrifying particular spots of the brain. It is more than probable that the two first of these experiments must have caused so severe a shock to the nervous system as to interfere materially with the results. It is not to be wondered at that a monkey's appetite should have been impaired after the whole of the occipital lobes of his brain had been removed. It is more reasonable to suppose that it was the shock of the operation which caused the lessened appetite rather than the injury to an imaginary seat of hunger, as Dr. Ferrier suggested. Neither can we place much reliance on the class of experiments which have reference to electrifying particular spots in the brain supposed to be the seats of sensation and motion.

---

* The first, *The Functions of the Brain*, was published in 1876. The second, *The Localisation of Cerebral Disease*, in 1878.
† *Vide The Journal of Psychological Medicine*, vol. iii., part II., and vol. v., part I.

Even granting that the electrical current had been directed with extreme precision to the required spot, what is to prevent the current from becoming diffused through the brain and the blood in its capillaries, as water, a good conductor, enters so largely into the composition of both? If this should occur it would be impossible to determine what set of muscles would or would not be affected by the experiment. There is also another influence which must be taken into consideration—reflex action —which is likely to interfere with the accuracy of the electrical experiments.

The fact must not be lost sight of that the convolutions of the brain are a homogeneous sort of mass, and that one convolution resembles another, as to microscopical appearances and chemical elements, as much as one portion of the liver does another, and it would be as reasonable to map out the latter into separate divisions, when there are no visible lines of demarcation, as the former. The brain must therefore be considered to act as a whole.

As Dr. Ferrier is evidently unable to determine precisely the centres of the mere bodily functions of sensation and motion, all that he has said in his chapter on *The Hemispheres considered Psychologically*** is so much waste paper.

With the unphilosophic haste so conspicuous in the materialistic school, it was most confidently asserted that the faculty of speech was located in the third frontal convolution of the left hemisphere of the brain, but this opinion has been proved to be incorrect by pathological facts. This localisation of the faculty of speech (Broca's theory) was the only ground which appeared to give any support to the materialists in their untiring efforts to destroy the independence of the human mind. Although this has been utterly swept away, as we shall presently show, they still cling with desperate energy to their forlorn hope.

Many cases are on record in which Broca's convolution and the island of Reil have been diseased or injured without loss of the faculty of speech. On the other hand, aphasia has been present when disease has been confined to the right side. To explain this contradictory evidence Broca suggests a most fanciful theory—that the faculty of speech is in some way connected with the use of the right side of the body and the left side of the brain.

One of the most striking instances adverse to the theory of a left-sided faculty of speech is the celebrated American crowbar case, in which a tamping iron an inch and quarter in diameter was driven completely through the head of a workman

---

* In his work on *The Functions of the Brain.*

by a sudden explosion of gunpowder. It was proved by careful measurement that it must have destroyed not only the left Sylvian artery, which supplies Broca's convolution, but also nearly the whole of the island of Reil. This extensive injury was not followed by any impairment of the faculty of speech.

A somewhat analogous case occurred in the practice of the late Mr. Lanyon, of Camborne, many years since. I had the particulars from himself, and he was a man of remarkable intelligence and undoubted veracity. A miner, whilst engaged in blasting a rock, was, by a sudden explosion, struck by a tamping iron, which entered at his forehead and came out at the back of his head, completely transfixing the brain. Incredible as it may appear, the man, soon after the accident, came to Mr. Lanyon's house, and in his presence tried to pull out the iron himself. This case was related to me long before the subject of aphasia was broached, or I should have made particular inquiries as to the man's mental condition, and as to which side the iron entered. As it is probable that the man was able to give an account of the accident, he could not have been aphasic; it is also more than likely that such an extensive lesion must have injured one or other of the anterior lobes of the brain.

For the future there will be no necessity for the advocates of Broca's theory to shift about from left to right, as the question has been set to rest by a crucial test. M. Bouillaud offered a prize of five hundred francs for any well-authenticated case in which the two anterior lobes were destroyed without speech being affected. This was claimed by M. Velpeau,* who had a patient under his care in whom a prominent symptom was *intolerable loquacity.* After death, it was found that a cancerous tumour had taken the place of the *two* anterior lobes.

Another case is recorded by M. Peter, of a man, who, after rallying from the first effects of a fracture of the skull, became extremely talkative. After death, it was discovered that the two anterior lobes were reduced to a pulp.

In 1877 I published† a case which occurred at St. Mary's Hospital, in which speech and memory continued after extensive softening of both anterior lobes of the brain.

Maragliano, one of the most strenuous advocates for experiments on the brain, only ventures to say modestly, that he thinks they will have a *tendency* towards the discovery of some general truth. Professor Pansch, of Keil, moreover, one of the late writers on the subject, is entirely opposed to division of the

---

* *Vide Gazette des Hopitaux* from April 6 to June 8, 1865, for the discussions on this case. It is remarkable that Dr. Ferrier never referred to this case in his work on *The Functions of the Brain.*

† *Vide Journal of Psychological Medicine*, vol. iv., part I.

brain into lobes, and proposes that it should be divided into principal convolutions, and these again into smaller sulci, and gyri.

Notwithstanding all the irrepressible facts we have just mentioned, Dr. Ferrier has published his materialistic and factless fancies in an article in the *Princeton Gazette** for July 1879, entitled *The Organ of Mind*, and there he makes the astounding and positive assertion, that it is " the brain that thinks . . . in connection with the whole sensory and nervous apparatus !" This is a *petitio principii* fallacy—the bane of modern science.

One of the miserable consequences of physiological psychology is, that having no sound fundamental principles for its basis, it involves its disciples in inextricable confusion of ideas, and entanglement of words. This is still further illustrated by the following remark of Dr. Ferrier's in the same article : " Mental phenomena are the subjective aspect of the functions of sensory and motor substrata, and that, in the last analysis, mental phenomena, however complex, should be reducible to correlation with the activity of certain simple motor and sensory elements, their accompaniments and combinations." In the vain attempt to cross the chasm which separates mind from matter, Dr. Ferrier became giddy in his flight, and has fallen down hopelessly crippled and confounded.

Unfortunately, the propagandism of physiological psychology does not end with Dr. Ferrier. In the *Nineteenth Century* for December 1879 Dr. Althaus, in speaking of the localisation of the faculty of intelligent language in the third left frontal convolution of the brain and its immediate neighbourhood, says : " This discovery was foreshadowed by Gall but *actually made* by Broca " ! One of the proofs of the truth of this discovery is, that when "electricity is applied to this part in the brain of the living monkey or rabbit the animal opens its mouth, and alternately obtrudes and retracts its tongue," in its efforts, we presume, to say, Don't.

Dr. Andrew Wilson, in an article on *The Old Phrenology and the New*, in the *Gentleman's Magazine* for January 1879, says : " Our 'New Phenology'—for the word is perfectly explicit as denoting a science of *mind* or brain—is gradually being built up from sure data and *accurate experimentation*."

Another publication, *Mind*, established a few years since,

---

* We have no fear that the Americans, who are a clear-headed and practical people, should take Dr. Ferrier's assertions for facts. We are convinced of this by an admirable *jeu d'esprit* which appeared not long since in an American paper. It described with an ingenious air of truth and scientific minuteness a wonderful instrument called a *cerebroscope*, by which the learned inventor could see the thoughts and sentiments as they arose in the brain. The account of the invention was copied into *The Journal of Psychological Medicine*, vol. v., part II.

has been doing its utmost to propagate the baneful doctrines of physiological psychology and positivism; but fortunately, owing to the dreary dulness of its articles, it is not likely to become popular. In the number for April 1879, there is a paper by Mr. Stavely Hall on the oft-told but ever-interesting story of Laura Bridgman, from which he flatters himself that he can gather facts in support of the views of his school. He has been unfortunate in his selection of this case. Blind, deaf, and dumb as she was from infancy, she learnt to communicate with the outer world by the means of the sense of touch alone, and it was observed that when dreaming, or thinking earnestly, her fingers moved like the lips of a person in deep thought. This shows the independent working of the human mind.

In the course of his disquisition, Mr. Stavely Hall makes the following incomprehensible remarks:—" Dreaming and waking notions are related as *species* and *genera*"; and he says of the sleeping state, " Inner work has brought *cells* [of the brain] into unstable equilibrium, and excitability very easily becomes excitation. Where the work of repair is not done, the slight stimuli of the sleeping state is not sufficient to rouse them ; where it is done, the almost *spontaneous activity of rested cells* easily raises *their processes above the threshold of consciousness.*" This is the sort of nonsense that is talked nowaday in the name of science and philosophy.

The *Edinburgh Review* for January 1879, in an article on *Mental Physiology*, has endorsed some of the boldest and most extravagant views of the materialistic physiologists. The writer, in referring to the recent experiments of Hitzig, Fritsch, Ferrier, and others, of trying to determine by electricity the centres of motion in the brain, observes : " There can be no doubt that in these experiments *ideas* were excited in the brains of the *insensible* animals by the physical agency of electrical currents. The brain-convolutions in reality consist of a number of distinct *mind-centres,* spread out in a kind of vault over the subordinate centres of nerve-action, which have the charge of consciousness, and are arranged layer above layer." What a boon this will be to a poor author, who has to cater weekly for the gratification of the public, to find that when his ideas are exhausted he can command a fresh supply by passing electric currents through his brain ! He goes so far as to say that the sensory ganglia take *cognisance* of sensuous impressions and also of mental states, thus endowing brain cells with the mental faculty of cognisance. He also says that the *brain substance* itself accomplishes the task of transmuting the impressions of sense *into ideas.* The term *idea* has always been regarded as synonymous with thought or conception ; they are among the highest manifestations of the mind, and as yet it has been found impossible to account for them by any physical laws. Further, he draws the following conclusions from what he considers the recent progress in scientific discovery: that, "with every expression of a *mental* state, and with every action of the *mind*, some structural change occurs in the substance of the brain."

We must protest against the acceptance of this hypothesis as an absolute truth. Had the question at stake been less momentous than that of the immateriality of the mind its dissemination might have been of little consequence; but when the issue is so tremendous, it is right that the general public, for whom the editor of the *Edinburgh* writes, and who cannot be expected to be familiar with the principles of a recondite and intricate science, should be cautioned against accepting mere speculations as verified facts.

A brief consideration of the writer's conclusion will be sufficient to show that it is, another striking example of the *petitio principii* fallacy. Neither the writer nor anyone else has demonstrated that with every act of the intellect some structural change occurs in the substance of the brain; that mind-action is the result of chemical decomposition of brain-pulp, or that the transmission of mind-force between the several globules of the brain is effected in the same manner. The brain is confined in a bony case which renders it impossible to watch its vital operations through the microscope. We must wait until the "cerebroscope" is realised before the physiologists can be in a position to speak positively on the point.

Dr. Allman in his address, at the meeting of the British Association at Sheffield, made a similar psychological blunder as the critic in the *Edinburgh Review.* He said when a thought passed through the mind it is associated, as we have now abundant reason for believing, with some change in the protoplasm of the cerebral cells. The *fact* is that we are not yet in possession of data to substantiate such an assertion, and it is of the utmost importance that a hasty opinion should not be formed on a question so closely associated with the independence of the human mind. This bold assertion, which has been accepted by many as an established truth, is the keynote of those who style themselves physiological psychologists, and whose endeavour it is to materialise mental phenomena, and identify mind with matter. In our waking moments it has never been demonstrated that a thought effects any change in the protoplasm of ganglionic cells of the brain; how utterly inconceivable it is then, that a subtle intangible thought, such as flits across the mind in a dream, should produce the slightest molecular alteration, especially at the very time when the nervous system is recuperating itself by rest, and is supposed to be least susceptible to impressions!

The doctrine of a correlation of force gives no support to physiological psychology: Grove's doctrine is applied most loosely. There is no evidence to show, as many assert, that mental, vital, and physical forces are identical. There is strong ground for believing that Grove's doctrine of the correlation of force applies to heat, electricity, chemical affinity, and motion; but there is no proof that it can be extended to mental or vital phenomena. Before a correlation of forces can be admitted, it is necessary, according to Mr. Justice Grove's explanation, to prove a mutual convertibility—a see-saw sort of action. Thus heat may mediately or immediately produce electricity, electricity may produce heat. With a total disregard of this clear statement, modern writers speak of the correlation (forgetting to add the word "force") of leaves and roots, of mental and nerve force, of vital and physical force, &c. If we apply the test of Grove's theory to the consideration of vital phenomena, we shall not find that a single instance has been recorded in which vital and physical force have been found interchangeable.

In the present day it is the practice of many scientific writers to use the terms correlation, evolution, and potentiality, to account for things that they cannot explain. They are used in a sort of hocus-pocus fashion. For instance, if it is asked, How did man originate?—the ready answer is, By evolution. What is life?—The potentiality of atoms. What is mind?—A correlation of magnetic and psychic forces.

The phenomena of insanity have been referred to on insufficient grounds by materialistic physiologists in proof of their theory. They refer to those particular cases of mental derangement in which marked signs of brain disease have been discovered after death. They also regard the beneficial effects which often result from physical remedies, as confirming this view. That bodily disorders will affect the mind is unquestioned, but the converse is equally true, that mental causes will produce derangement of the bodily organs; and the physiological psychologists are asked to explain how it happens that in many cases of acute mania, ending rapidly in death, a *post-mortem* examination cannot detect any change in the substance of the brain. The decided influence of the mind on the body is, however, patent to the most superficial observer. Is there any cordial like hope to the poor sufferer prostrated by nervous depression from domestic or other mental anxiety? Or, will not some moral shock, such as the sudden announcement of misfortune or bereavement, shattering all hope of worldly prosperity or home happiness, convert a healthy man into a raving lunatic?

All those who have resided much with the insane can bear witness to the intelligence and accomplishments frequently observed in patients suffering from incurable brain disease, and to the lighting up of the mind during the last moments of life. One case especially occurs to me, that of an old lady who was formerly under my care. She had passed the greater part of her life in an asylum, and during that period had never been for a moment coherent, yet just before her dissolution she spoke quite sensibly.

It is a well-known fact that in uncomplicated cases of acute mania, where death ensues rapidly from exhaustion, a *post mortem* examination detects no change in the *substance* of the brain, although the membrane may be congested, a common occurrence not peculiar to insanity. Again, in cases of *mania transitoria*, how is it possible to associate the delirium, which lasts only a few hours, with lesion of the brain?

The phenomena of dreaming, which closely resembles some forms of insanity, may be noticed here. The analogy between the phantasms of the one and the hallucinations of the other is very remarkable, and the rival schools of the subjectivists and objectivists both claim these phenomena as evidence of the truth of their respective theories. To us it appears that the balance of the arguments are on the side of the subjective view, for what can be less material than "the stuff that dreams are made of"? In dreams, when the mind is uninfluenced by external impressions, it is left to wander fancy free among the images and memories of the past. Consciousness and memory are not lost, and the emotions and imagination are in full force.

The most obscure problem connected with sleep and dreaming, and the one respecting which there are such conflicting opinions, is that which relates to the state of the mind in what is called dreamless sleep. Some assert that at such times the mind is a perfect blank; others, as it appears to me, with more probability, that the profoundest sleep is not unattended with dreams, though sometimes they are as utterly forgotten as if they had never occurred.

With a view of throwing light upon the question of the subjectivity of dreams, and of ascertaining whether the images which occur in sleep are viewed by the "mind's eye," after long deprivation of sight, or are merely automatic excitations of a sense surface, I sought the experience of Dr. W. A. F. Browne, of Dumfries, who has been blind for seven years. No living psychologist is more competent to give an opinion on this abstruse subject. He kindly sent me the following analysis of his mental state during sleep, with permission to publish it. He observes : " I have been blind for seven years, and being of a nervous active temperament, there has been a continuous stream of thought presented to consciousness. These thoughts have consisted mainly, but not exclusively, in the reproduction of former impressions. First, I have never experienced recollections of taste, smell, rarely of touch ; frequently of hearing, and necessarily of vision. These impressions refer in great measure to past time, and to the earlier portions of my life ; but a vast portion do not. I have long since rejected the photographic hypothesis. Secondly, because the mental conditions are entirely new to myself ; they are discoveries, creations. Thirdly, where this is not the case, and these conditions are combinations of familiar and unknown scenes or impressions, it is obvious that the act of uniting them into a congruous whole cannot be the effect of volition or any conscious mental operation, and is utterly inconsistent with any photographic manipulation, or the fortuitous union of a hundred photographs. Fourthly, independently altogether of visual impressions, emotions and sentiments are experienced during sleep, such as fear or hope, which may or may not be the natural results of the existing mental state, and which cannot, in any sense, be of photographic origin. Fifthly, it is worthy of note that, however distant the period at which the impressions may have been received, say in early childhood, it is invariably the present Ego which sees it, hears it, and is identified with it."

The new phrenologists having settled, to their own satisfaction, that each faculty of the mind has a special seat of its own in which to carry on its operations, it only remained to explain its *modus operandi*. Each centre is supposed to be under the control of a number of brain-cells—a sort of limited liability company of molecules—which alone is responsible for any evil thoughts it may engender. This little hypothesis only requires us to assume, in the first place, that each cell is endowed with mental attributes. This resembles the theory of Leibnitz—that monads had perceptions and appetites.

It has never been proved that the cells of the brain are exempt from that law of constant renewal which generally obtains in the soft tissues of the body. The probability is, from its delicate texture, that it is constantly in need of renovation. Its fragility is conspicuous after death, for it is a fact familiar to every student of anatomy, that it is one of the very first parts of the body that decomposes. If, then, the brain be of such a perishable nature, it is incredible that images or ideas impressed by any merely physical process on the cells of the brain could be vividly recalled after a long period of time, when the matter of the very cells which were supposed to have received them had been replaced by new matter.

The last subject of physiological psychology we propose to notice is that of unconscious cerebration ; it need not detain us long. The supposed function of the brain was announced as a new discovery by Dr. Carpenter. It assumed that the human brain is capable of carrying on trains of reasoning, of drawing conclusions and forming *conscious* ideas without *consciousness* ; in fact, that the higher faculties of the mind can be exercised independently of the mind itself! If this were true, it would reduce all human beings to mere automata; a very pleasant creed for those who dislike mental labour, as it is supposed to do a great deal of our thinking without any trouble to ourselves, like the working of a steam engine.

Another incomprehensible notion allied to unconscious cerebration, is, what the advanced physiologists have named *ideo-motor* actions, involuntarily performed under the direction of ideas. As, therefore, the former relieves us from all responsibility as to our thoughts, so the latter exonerates us from all the blame of evil actions. Very comfortable doctrines these for those who desire to follow the bent of vicious inclinations without let or hindrance. The chief facts which gave rise to these theories are those connected with walking, and with the rapid movements of an accomplished musician's hands; and the singular manner in which a person recalls to his memory a word or thought that seemed utterly forgotten. As regards the first, it is probable that when a command over any particular set of muscles has been obtained, the amount of attention given to the direction of the movements is so small, and the recognition of it so faint, as to escape the memory. The second instance may be accounted for by the laws of mental association.

A strong indication that physiological psychology has broken down, is evinced by the circumstance that Dr. Hughlings-Jackson, one of its leading authorities and most strenuous supporters, is at length compelled to admit that metaphysics and physics are distinct branches of science, and must be kept apart. He writes in the *Medical Press* for September 3, 1879 : " In a scientific investigation of nervous diseases, it is essential *to keep distinct psychology* and the anatomy and *physiology* of the nervous system. . . . I have been misled by not having seen the distinctness of physical (nervous) states and psychical states,* in my earlier studies, and thus *I feel bold* to point out the evil

* Another puzzled materialist, writing in the *British Medical Journal* for November 8, 1879, flatters himself that he can get out of the difficulty by substituting the term psychological physiology for physiological psychology. " Strange such difference should be 'twixt tweedledum and tweedledee."

results of the *confusion of the two things.*" Dr. Hughlings-Jackson must not think that he has acted with extraordinary boldness in making these remarks. He has not been the first to mount the breach. I pointed out the fallacies of physiological psychology in an article on *Materialistic Physioloy* in vol. iii., new series, of the *Journal of Psychological Medicine.*

The modern cerebral physiologists have been guilty of a serious and culpable error in their attempt to explain mental phenomena by a hasty generalisation from the very few facts that are known respecting the nature and properties of the ganglionic cells so extensively diffused throughout the cortical substance of the brain. The mind is an entity—a first principle—and it is as unphilosophical as it is inconceivable that matter should think.

Their hasty and illogical conclusions would have mattered comparatively but little, if the question at issue had reference only to physical science; but when their haphazard speculations tend to shake a belief in the independence of the human mind—a belief that has been upheld by the greatest philosophers both of ancient and modern times—they might surely have hesitated before enunciating doctrines which, if true, would make man an irresponsible agent and sap the foundations of morality and religion.

From all the facts that have been adduced, it must be patent to every unprejudiced inquirer that physical force cannot account for life; that neither bathybius nor spontaneous generation can explain the origin of bioplasm; that our first parents were not grovelling savages; that evolution is not the First Cause; that physiological psychology has not solved the mystery of the human mind; and that, when tested by the irrepressible, inextinguishable, irresistible, inexorable logic of facts, the pseudo-philosophy of scientific atheism collapses—ignominiously collapses.—Q.E.D.

Spottiswoode & Co., Printers, New-street Square, London.